Police Dog Recruit

Story and Concept by
Andy Falco and Kelly Falco

Illustrated by
Jolie Chevaun

Copyright © 2015 by Andy Falco/Kelly Falco

All rights reserved. No part of this publication may be reproduced, distributed, or transmitted in any form or by any means, including photocopying, recording, or other electronic or mechanical methods, without the prior written permission of the publisher, except in the case of brief quotations embodied in critical reviews and certain other noncommercial uses permitted by copyright law. For permission requests, write to the publisher, addressed "Attention: Permissions Coordinator," at the address below.

Tactical Productions and Marketing
4691 Valley View Avenue
Yorba Linda, CA 92886
www.TacticalProductionsAndMarketing.com - 714-990-9010

Ordering Information:
Quantity sales. Special discounts are available on quantity purchases by child related corporations, associations, and others (at the description of the authors). For details, contact the publisher at the address above.

Printed in the United States of America

Introduction

One day my son Kelly and I were preparing for bed time. As many parents do, my wife and I read books to our kids. Sometimes I make up stories and sometimes I tell them stories about when I was a police officer and police K9 handler with the City of Anaheim, California. On one special night my son Kelly was begging me to tell him a story about when I was a K9 handler with my police K9 partner Falco von Aramis. But instead I wanted to have a discussion. I asked Kelly, "If you were to read a book about my police dog, what would you want to read in that book." And this book is a result of that conversation. Kelly told me he would want to know where the dog came from and how the dog became a police dog. He wanted to know about how the dog uses his nose solve crime. And how the dog knows the odor of the suspect is different then anyone else's odor.

As we talked we realized that "if we were to write a book," the book would have to be written for both children and the adults who read to them. This way we could keep it readable for new readers while also giving the adults adequate information to explain in more detail to the children as they asked the very same questions Kelly had asked me. As you will see there is large print in simple to read sentences for young readers and listeners. In smaller print on the same page you will see a deeper discussion that coincides with the story. And of course you will see beautifully illustrated pictures that go along with the story. Thank you to our illustrator Jolie Chevaun.

Forward

Kelly Falco (Son, 8 years old):

First of all, I am so thankful for the time I have with my dad. It is so fun to hear his stories about being a police officer and the stories of working with his police dog. It was fun working on this story together.

I am happy that other children will learn about police dogs and how they protect us and find dangerous things we could never find without them. I am also happy you will learn why we use dogs; what breeds are used for police work and how they are able to use their nose to find bad guys. I think it is amazing how they know the difference from the bad guy's odor and other people's odor… that is crazy to me.

I hope you like our book. My dad and I have more stories for you about other working dogs. And maybe my brothers and sisters will join us in writing more books. What do you think?

Falco is a German Shepherd. He dreams of becoming a Police Dog. His father and grandfather were Police Dogs.

German Shepherds are usually seen in movies and TV as Police K9s. But other breeds of dogs are also used by law enforcement. Belgian Malinois and Rottweilers are used when searching for dangerous suspects because they are large, fast and strong. Labrador Retrievers and similar breeds are used to detect narcotics and explosives because of their desire to play and friendliness.

Dogs who are trained to be Police Dogs need strong personality traits and good genetics to do the job effectively. The offspring of Police Dogs are often chosen for the same type of work.

To help him achieve his goal of becoming a Police Dog, Falco always listens to his mom and dad and does his best to stay out of trouble.

It's natural for dogs to learn from other dogs, especially young pups from older members of a pack. At Falco K9 Academy, veteran dogs show the "rookies" the difficult behaviors and skills needed for police work.

All dogs should be taught obedience and to follow rules and respect boundaries—just as it's important to set rules and boundaries for children. It's really a balance of Love and Respect between children and their parents, just as it's Love and Respect between dogs and their humans.

"To grow up strong and smart, you must eat right and get plenty of sleep," says Falco's mom. So he goes to bed when he's told.

Rest and sleep are keys to proper mental and physical development for humans. It's no different for dogs. When training dogs for any discipline (patrol work, detection, search & rescue), the time for rest is JUST AS IMPORTANT as the training process.

When training a dog, don't forget these rules:
1. Keep training short
2. End the session on success
3. Give reasonable time for the dog to rest in a quiet place away from distractions

Vegetables aren't his favorite food, but Falco's dream is more important, so he eats well.

Good nutrition is essential for working dogs AND pet dogs. A healthy diet includes protein like fowl, lamb, and beef, as well as vegetables and other necessary nutrients. Don't forget to change it up once in a while—dogs deserve variety too! Some dogs have dietary requirements or other considerations, so consult a veterinarian before making drastic diet changes.

It's also crucial to maintain a dog's proper weight. Overfeeding can lead to obesity, and that extra weight is harmful to joints. Large breed dogs are prone to hip and shoulder problems, so feed them properly.

Falco loves to hear tales that his dad and grandfather tell about their time on the police force.

Learning from past experiences is a vital part of training service dogs. It's necessary to learn from other trainers and share stories of success and failure.

Sharing your life experiences with your kids in a way that's both fun and educational is a part of effective parenting. Also, invite your children to share the things that concern and scare them. There's nothing more important than knowing your child's friends, interests, and fears.

Now would be a great time to take a break from the story and ask your child what he/she wants to know about you.

Falco uses his powerful nose to search for imaginary bad guys who leave the scene of a crime. A dog's ability to smell is a million times better than a human's.

A dogs nose is incredibly powerful. Because of their almost "supernatural" ability we use dogs to search for things that are dangerous to our health and safety and that includes "bad guys". Dogs can literally smell the ground and determine where someone has walked. The dog smells both the ground disturbance that occurs with each step combined with the odor that falls off an individual's body as they walk. The dogs olfactory (nasal area) system has the ability to smell minute particles of odor AND it separate the odors. This allows them to locate the odor they are trained to find very easily and allows us to use them to save lives and catch "bad guys". It is truly incredible.

Every chance Falco gets, he plays hard and works hard to learn to be a good Police Dog. He runs, jumps, and pretends to solve crimes.

It's important to get plenty of exercise and stimulate our brains no matter how young or old we are. Kelly (the co-author) loves to play hockey, ride his skateboard, and play football with his dad, Andy (the other co-author). He also goes on nature walks with his mom to look for insects, plants, and animals to identify and write about in a journal. Andy also likes to play hockey and do all the things his kids love to do.

Falco and his sister Fiona play a game called "Evidence." Fiona hides his favorite toy, then Falco searches for it using only his nose.

To be considered for a patrol or detection dog, a dog is given a test of finding its toy. For example, the toy is hidden in a room or field. The dog is then told to go find it. The trainers watch as the dog smells the ground and air to locate the toy's odor. A dog passes the test by effectively searching for and locating the toy without giving up.

One day, Falco and Fiona go for a walk with their humans. They see local police and two men in handcuffs.

As a Police Officer, I (Andy) often stopped suspects that I thought had just committed a crime, or they matched the description given by witnesses. The problem was that I couldn't always connect the suspects to the crime or crime scene. That's where Police Dogs helped. With their superior noses, they'd often lead me to evidence or the actual "fruits" of the crime (tools, money, weapons) and link the people I had detained with the crime. Without the dogs, I wouldn't have been able to nab the bad guys.

Falco smells the men seated on the ground. Their scent is unique and different than the other human beings.

Little does Falco know that the police don't have all the evidence needed to arrest the men whom they believe robbed a bank.

Every human has a unique odor. To a dog, that odor is as unique as a fingerprint is to law enforcement. Some of the reasons a person's odor is unique is due to genetics, gender, deodorant, soap, clothing detergent and food eaten. This is why a dog can differentiate between one person and the next.

It may sound like a "fairy tail" that dogs can pick up the odor of an individual and follow it to determine a connection to a crime. But this is how dogs are used in law enforcement everyday. Dogs follow the track (odor and ground disturbance) from suspects back to the scene of the crime. This fantastic ability of dogs is used to solve many crimes.

As he walks away, Falco can't stop thinking about the smell of the two men in handcuffs.

All dogs know how to follow a track, such as to find a cat, chase a squirrel, or locate its owner. But to train a dog to follow a random human track from beginning to end (sometimes for hundreds of yards or miles) takes a very special dog. It's important to find dogs who from a young age have been properly selected and trained to follow a human track for human purposes.

Children must be properly trained from a young age as well to prepare them for a happy and productive life. As parents, we should encourage good habits of nutrition, socialization, study, and honesty in our kids. We should also be aware of their likes and dislikes, know who their friends are, and stay active in their development.

Suddenly, Falco smells something. It's the same smell as the men in handcuffs. Falco sniffs the air and follows the odor to a bush next to the bank . . . the same bank that was robbed! The smell of the odor gets stronger as Falco sticks his head in the bush.

Everyone who has owned a dog has seen the dog search for something with its nose and become excited when it discovers where it's located. For Police Dog handlers, this moment is one of the most rewarding parts of the job. When a dog finds evidence that police never would have been able to find, it makes all the hard work and training worthwhile.

During my career with the Anaheim Police Department, my Police Dog found over 100 suspects with his "supernatural" nose and abilities.

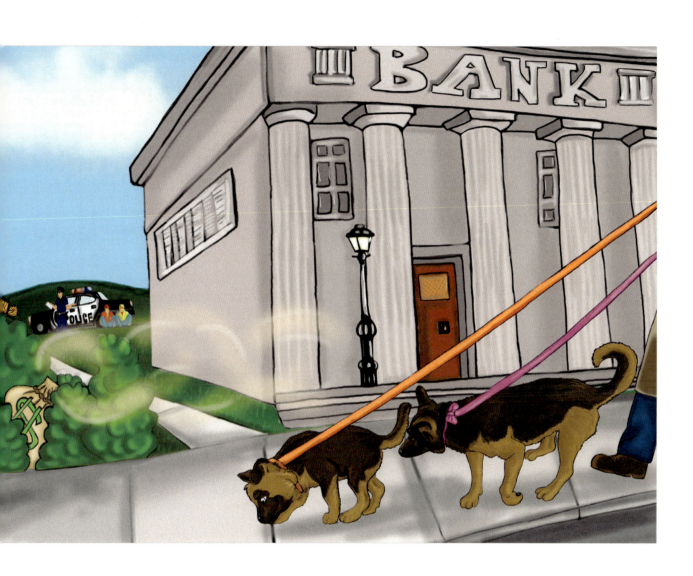

Falco looks inside the bush and sees a bag with money. It smells just like the men in handcuffs. Falco barks to alert the police.

One of the most useful abilities of a Police Dog is their ability to locate and alert to evidence in a crime. This can be a gun, knife, or screwdriver. Once a person touches anything, his/her odor is left behind on that object. The odor stays on the object for several days and sometimes months, depending on the type of surface.

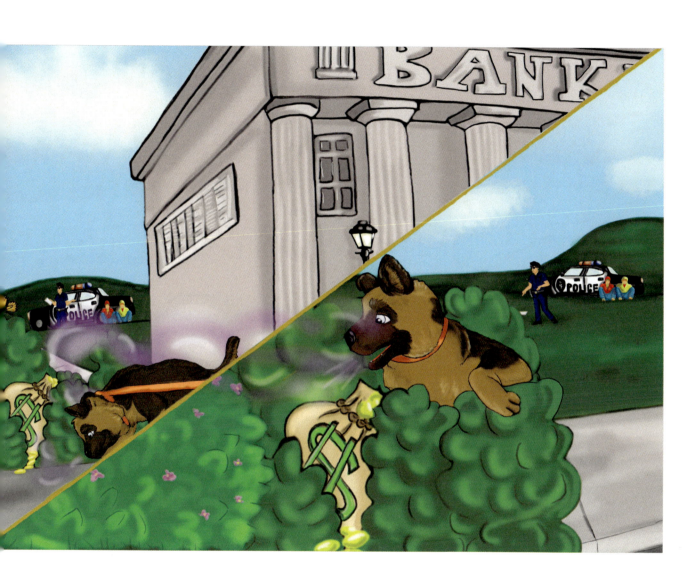

The police run to Falco. They look inside the bush and find the missing money and gun used in the robbery. This is all the police officers need to arrest the two men. Thanks to Falco, the crime is solved!

To place a person under arrest, a law enforcement officer needs what is called probable cause and/or solid evidence. Because a properly trained police dog's nose is so powerful and reliable, courts accept evidence gained through the use of a Police Dog. Because of this, it's important to always search for the best of the best of dogs and train them properly.

Falco receives an honorary badge from the police department for being a Police K9 for a day.

A dog does not have to be a Police Dog to assist humans. Dogs have been domesticated since the early history of man in order to help people. They alert us to dangers, provide protection, help hunt, and serve as companions.

What does your dog do for you?

Falco thanks his family for all they've done to help him prepare for his day as a Police K9. He is on his way to becoming a REAL Police K9.

It's never too late to thank people in your life who helped you succeed. Teach your children to be thankful for what they have and for those who are mentors to them.

Also, don't forget to reward your dog when it does something right. It's easy to focus on the things it does that are bad. You will have much better relationships with humans and dogs if you focus on and reward the good.

Made in the USA
Middletown, DE
12 October 2023

40699992R00022